# PHARRELL WILLIAMS

**by K.C. Kelley**

Consultant: Starshine Roshell
Music and Entertainment Journalist
Santa Barbara, CA

BEARPORT
PUBLISHING

New York, New York

Publisher: Kenn Goin
Creative Director: Spencer Brinker
Production and Photo Research: Shoreline Publishing Group LLC

Library of Congress Cataloging-in-Publication Data

Names: Kelley, K. C., author.
Title: Pharrell Williams / by K.C. Kelley.
Description: New York, New York : Bearport Publishing, [2018] | Series:
    Amazing Americans: pop music stars | Includes bibliographical references
    and index.
Identifiers: LCCN 2017045544 (print) | LCCN 2017045589 (ebook) |
    ISBN 9781684025152 (ebook) | ISBN 9781684024575 (library)
Subjects: LCSH: Williams, Pharrell—Juvenile literature. | Rap
    musicians—United States—Biography—Juvenile literature.
Classification: LCC ML3930.W55 (ebook) | LCC ML3930.W55 K45 2018 (print) |
    DDC 782.421649092 [B]—dc23
LC record available at https://lccn.loc.gov/2017045544

For more information, write to Bearport Publishing Company, Inc., 45 West 21st Street, Suite 3B, New York, New York 10010. Printed in the United States of America.

10 9 8 7 6 5 4 3 2 1

# CONTENTS

# Music Lover!

Pharrell (fuh-RELL) Williams is a music superstar. He's a singer, a songwriter, and a performer. He also helps others create songs and albums. He inspires millions with his catchy **lyrics**.

Pharrell was a coach on the TV talent show *The Voice* from 2014 to 2016.

Pharrell performs in England in 2015.

# Early Years

Pharrell Lanscilo Williams was born on April 5, 1973, in Virginia Beach, Virginia. He was musical from a very young age. Pharrell's grandmother convinced him to join a band class at age six. He used her pots and pans as a drum set!

Pharrell played keyboards and drums in band class.

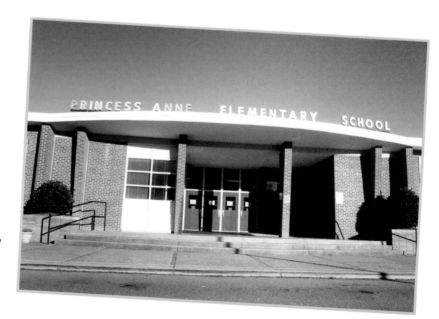

Pharrell's school, Princess Anne Elementary

Growing up, Pharrell often visited this oceanside pier in his hometown.

# Pharrell's First Band

Pharrell met Chad Hugo in seventh grade. They were both in the school marching band. In high school, the boys formed an **R&B** band called The Neptunes. This was the start of Pharrell's amazing musical career.

**Pharrell as a high school senior**

In the marching band, Chad was the drum major.

Chad and Pharrell are still friends. They went to this Los Angeles event together in 2016.

9

# First Break

The Neptunes played in a high school talent show. Record **producer** Teddy Riley saw the band perform. He loved their music! Soon after, Teddy gave The Neptunes a record deal.

Teddy Riley's recording studio was close to Pharrell's house. The young singer could walk there!

Teddy Riley

Pharrell and Chad (on keyboard) performing together

# The Big Hit

Pharrell and Chad began producing music together. They also helped other singers and musicians. In 1992, Pharrell helped write a new song. It reached number two on the *Billboard* Hot 100 list. Soon, everyone wanted to know about these young, creative stars.

**Pharrell shows off a sneaker he designed.**

Pharrell sings with Jay-Z at a concert in Canada in 2009.

Pharrell and Hugo have made songs with music stars, including Jay-Z, Diddy, and Usher.

# Gaining Fame

Pharrell and Hugo's first album, *The Neptunes Present . . . Clones*, came out in 2003. That year, the two musicians won their first **Grammy** Award. It was for producing other artists' songs. Later, Pharrell also performed during the Grammy Awards.

As of 2017, Pharrell has won 11 Grammy Awards.

Pharrell performs
during the 2014 Grammys
with Stevie Wonder.

# Pharrell Goes Solo

In 2006, Pharrell made his first solo album. It was called *In My Mind*. It was a success. Still, Pharrell missed working with his friends. He returned to producing songs with Hugo. That same year, they won a Grammy for Best **Rap** Song.

**Pharrell invited other artists to appear on *In My Mind*. They included Gwen Stefani (right), Jay-Z, Kanye West, and Nelly.**

Pharrell sings in Texas in 2008.

# A World Superstar

In 2013, Pharrell had a big year. He wrote and performed a song called "Happy." It was used in the movie *Despicable Me 2*. The song was a huge hit and became famous around the world. That summer, everyone was singing and dancing along to the catchy tune.

**Pharrell with a Minion from *Despicable Me 2*.**

Pharrell's big hat gets a lot of attention!

In 2016, Pharrell was nominated for an Oscar for producing the movie *Hidden Figures*.

# More Than Music

Pharrell is known for more than music. He loves fashion! Fans can't wait to see his interesting outfits. Pharrell's style inspires many people. However, his first loves will always be his family—and music!

Pharrell got a star on the Hollywood Walk of Fame in California in 2014.

Pharrell and his wife, Helen, and their son Rocket

Pharrell owns a clothing and art company called i am OTHER.

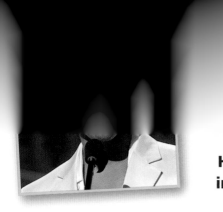

## Here are some key dates in Pharrell Williams's life.

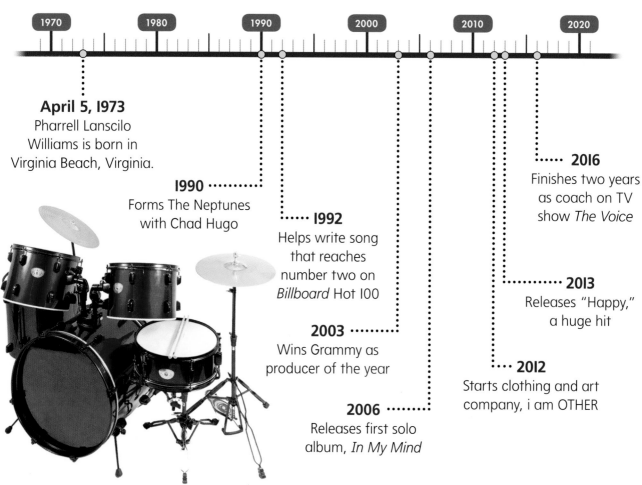

1970 — 1980 — 1990 — 2000 — 2010 — 2020

**April 5, 1973**
Pharrell Lanscilo Williams is born in Virginia Beach, Virginia.

**1990**
Forms The Neptunes with Chad Hugo

**1992**
Helps write song that reaches number two on *Billboard* Hot 100

**2003**
Wins Grammy as producer of the year

**2006**
Releases first solo album, *In My Mind*

**2016**
Finishes two years as coach on TV show *The Voice*

**2013**
Releases "Happy," a huge hit

**2012**
Starts clothing and art company, i am OTHER

# Glossary

**drum major** (DRUM MAYJ-er) the leader of a marching band

**Grammy** (GRAMM-ee) an award that recognizes the best music each year

**lyrics** (LEER-iks) the words of a song

**producer** (pruh-DOO-ser) a person who records and arranges the music for a song

**rap** (RAPP) a type of music that includes a lot of rhyming words spoken quickly

**R&B** (ARR AND BEE) letters standing for rhythm and blues, a style of music

# Index

# Read More

**Flores, Christopher Lee.** *Pharrell Williams: Singer and Songwriter (Junior Biographies).* New York: Enslow (2017).

**Uhl, Xina M.** *Pharrell Williams: Music Industry Star (Superstar Stories).* Mankato, MN: Child's World (2017).

# Learn More Online

To learn more about Pharrell Williams, visit
**www.bearportpublishing.com/AmazingAmericans**

# About the Author

K.C. Kelley has written more than 100 books for young readers, including many on sports and lots of biographies.